THIS SIDE
UP

FAT CATS

F A T   C A T S

EDITED BY

J. C. SUARÈS

TEXT BY

H. D. R. CAMPBELL

PHOTO RESEARCH BY

KATRINA FRIED

WELCOME ENTERPRISES, INC.

NEW YORK

First published in 1997 by
Welcome Enterprises, Inc.
New York

Distributed by Stewart, Tabori & Chang, Inc.
a division of U.S. Media Holdings, Inc.
115 West 18th Street, New York, NY 10011
Distributed in Canada by General Publishing Co., Ltd.
30 Lesmill Road, Don Mills, Ontario, Canada M3B 2T6
Distributed in the U.K. by Hi Marketing
38 Carver Road, London SE24 9LT, United Kingdom
Distributed in Australia and New Zealand by Peribo Pty.
Ltd
58 Beaumont Road, Mount Kuring-gai NSW 2080, Australia

Library of Congress Card Catalog Number: 97-060493

ISBN 1-55670-682-0

Printed and bound in Italy

10 9 8 7 6 5 4 3 2 1

How do you get a picture of the biggest domestic feline in the world, a pleasant 46-pound house cat named Himmy? As I began my search, little did I know that Himmy would become the Holy Grail of fat cats, a cat of almost mythic importance in the world of overweight felines.

The first call was to the publisher of the *Guinness Book of World Records*. A brusque woman on the other end of the line informed me that they had ceased to be Guinness's publisher some years ago, and referred me elsewhere. As it goes, I was passed along from one person to another, until finally, over a dozen calls and two weeks later, I reached an incredibly decent young lady named Cecilia in London, who appeared to have access to all photographs appearing in Guinness's publications. Success!... Or maybe not. Two days later, after promising to look through the photo files personally, Cecilia called to very apologetically inform me that because *Guinness* was in the process of scanning all photographs onto computer, the pictures were unavailable for outside use until at least February of 1997. Foiled again. Fortunately, I was able to get the name of Himmy's photographer and a partial address: Cairns, Australia.

International information and a few lucky guesses helped me finally track down the exact address and phone number of the photographer. In my excitement, I immediately dialed the overseas number, only to receive a series of rings with no answer, human or mechanical. As I went to hang up the receiver in total defeat, a small voice caught my ear. "Allo...Who's there?" Even the thick Australian accent could not disguise the grogginess of the young man's voice. I raced to pull the handset back to my ear, simultaneously checking my watch, as I realized with horror that at 2 P.M. in New York it was 3 A.M. in Australia. Oops. "I am so sorry," I gushed," I didn't think…I woke you…I'll call back, okay?" Very professional-sounding. On the other end the sound of a hacking cough reverberated across oceans of phone line—the kind that could make even the most addicted smoker consider quitting. Clearing his throat, the man replied, "Who is this?" I managed to get out my name and reason for calling and the young man reluctantly agreed to let me call back the following morning to speak to his mother, not only the photographer of Himmy, but the owner as well.

I called back at precisely 9 A.M. the next day and talked with Doreen, the proudest cat mama you ever did meet. She spoke in the slow, deliberate manner of a woman who is both overly self-conscious of her heavy "Down-Under" dialect and weak from a recent illness. I listened as she described both her and Himmy's life (and declining health); how Himmy had an affinity for wheelbarrows and hugs and never let his fame go to his head. She offered to send me whatever pictures she had and asked only for a copy of this book in return. Needless to say, I was humbled.

The pictures of Himmy included in this book are those that found their way to me across oceans and continents in a tattered envelope covered in stamps with a carefully hand-printed return address: Cairns, Australia. Home of Himmy: The Fattest Cat in the World.

KATRINA FRIED

"The cat is a lion to the mouse."

ALBANIAN PROVERB
A Celebration of Cats

RIGHT:
ANTONÍN MALÝ
PRAGUE, CZECH REPUBLIC, 1996

"This fat cat starred in an exhibition I had in Prague
last year. He belongs to a good friend of mine."

PREVIOUS PAGES:
DOREEN AND THOMAS VYSE
CAIRNS, QUEENSLAND, AUSTRALIA, CIRCA 1986

"Himmy, 46 pounds 15.25 ounces, was like a person, not like a
cat; you could talk to him. Regarding weight, he never ate more
than eight to ten ounces of food a day. All of a sudden, he just
started to grow."

ABOVE:

ROBIN SCHWARTZ

BROOKLYN, NY, 1996

"Fat cat Walter loves to watch the water swirl in the toilet bowl.

RIGHT:

ROBIN SCHWARTZ

BROOKLYN, NY, 1996

Walter gets a big hug from his owner, Angela.

OVERLEAF:

JOHN DRYSDALE

HASLEMERE, ENGLAND, 1979

Marvin began life as a sickly kitten who was fed from an eyedropper. He grew up on a gourmet diet of venison, salmon from Scotland, steak, chicken, and vitamins with ice cream. Marvin refused all cat food and preferred a ride in the family's vintage chauffeur-driven car to chasing mice in the garden. Marvin always traveled on his own velvet cushion.

ROBIN SCHWARTZ
NEW YORK, NY, 1996

"This cat lives at Culver Pictures, a photo archive.
He looks as if he is smiling but actually, he's hissing;
he didn't care for the flash on my camera."

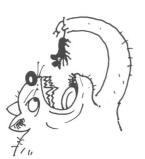

A cat I keep

that lays about my house

Grown fat with eating

Many a miching mouse.

ROBERT HERRICK

RIGHT:
THOMAS WESTER
KALMAR, SWEDEN, 1977

"This cat, Felicia, or Puppan in Swedish, had eaten her Christmas rice pudding and then settled in for a long snooze near the warm radiator. She weighs about thirteen pounds."

OVERLEAF:
THOMAS WESTER
STOCKHOLM, SWEDEN, 1990

"This fat cat loves to take sunbaths."

ABOVE:

PHOTOGRAPHER UNKNOWN
PARIS, FRANCE, 1963

At the annual show presented by the Cat Circle of
Paris, this Blue Persian makes his first appearance.
The cat's young mistress, however, thinks more of him
as a playmate than as a prospective champion.

(Original caption, circa 1963)

RIGHT:

PHOTOGRAPHER UNKNOWN
LONDON, ENGLAND, DATE UNKNOWN

Little Gordon Peters, two years old, carrying his Blue
Persian kitten, Minnow, into the Royal Horticultural Hall.

Only ten percent of cats are overweight, far fewer than the thirty percent of dogs. And life expectancy does not seem to be shortened significantly for these overweight cats…if a cat is happy and content to be overweight, that condition is not overwhelmingly harmful. Humans have a mania about fatness. In their culture, fat is a negative. Because they treat cats as members of their human family, they apply the "fat is bad" rule to their cats too. For a household feline it ain't necessarily so.

BRUCE FOGLE
101 Questions Your Cat Would Ask
Its Vet If Your Cat Could Talk

JIM DRATFIELD/PAUL COUGHLIN
NEW YORK, NY, 1996
"One look at Sparky, a gorgeous Himalayan, and I knew this fat cat was destined for feline stardom. He has appeared in two books and on a greeting card."

I once got a scare from a little cat of ours named Charlie.
I came into the kitchen and found him prostrate on his
stomach on the floor, breathing heavily. In a panic, I lifted
him gently and tried to get him to stand on his legs, but
they collapsed under him again. And as I supported him I
noticed that his stomach seemed bloated. I stood up, trying
to decide whether to telephone our veterinarian or rush
Charlie to the animal hospital emergency room, and then I
noticed something. Almost an entire platter of spaghetti with
clam sauce that had been on the counter had disappeared.
Charlie wasn't suffering from some terrible neurological
disorder—he'd simply OD'd on spaghetti, and his skinny
adolescent legs wouldn't support his overloaded stomach.

PATRICIA CURTIS
THE INDOOR CAT

THOMAS WESTER
STOCKHOLM, SWEDEN, 1984

Moses had several homes. Unfortunately, he lived with people
who turned out to be allergic to cats. He went from one foster
home to another until finally, he ended up in an aparment with
four girls who truly loved him. While moving from place to place,
Moses learned to console himself with food and became very
good at locating it. He probably weighed over fifteen pounds.

ROBIN SCHWARTZ
BROOKLYN, NY, MID-1980S

"Whitey [right] had been my
cat since I was ten years old.
He was my cat brother. I used to
sleep with him in my arms. On
trips Tobey [my other cat] rode in a
carrier, but it would have been an
insult to put Whitey in a cage."

ABOVE:

TONY MENDOZA

NEW YORK, NY, 1993

"This big white cat belonged to a neighbor.
I simply call him New York City cat."

RIGHT:

ELLIOTT ERWITT

PLACE UNKNOWN, 1975

"I don't always remember where I took a photograph.
I just take the picture and then forget about it. This is just
a cat lying on a patio table, but what a cat!"

OVERLEAF:

THOMAS WESTER

STOCKHOLM, SWEDEN, 1984

After a 621-mile flight to be mated,
this sly little puss changed her mind.

I saw the most beautiful cat today. It was sitting

by the side of the road, its two front feet neatly

and graciously together. Then it gravely swished

around its tail to completely and snugly encircle

itself. It was so fit and beautifully neat, that

gesture, and so self-satisfied—so complacent.

ANNE MORROW LINDBERGH
Bring Me A Unicorn: Diaries and Letters of
Anne Morrow Lindbergh, 1922-1928

THOMAS WESTER
STOCKHOLM, SWEDEN, 1984

A formidable fat cat who weighs in at 18.5
pounds, Mose strolls the streets of southern
Stockholm with nary a care for passing cars.
Once home, he patiently waits for someone to
let him into his apartment building. Inside he
knows another good samaritan will come along
and take him up in the elevator to his floor.

Cats are absolute individuals with

their own ideas about everything,

including the people they own.

JOHN DINGMAN
THE ARTISTIC CAT

RIGHT:
PHOTOGRAPHER UNKNOWN
PARIS, FRANCE, 1978

Vicky de Kerlutun, an international Persian
champion, won competitions in Brussels, Paris,
and Geneva. She was six years old in this
photograph and weighed in at over twelve pounds.

OVERLEAF:
ANN TOMLINSON FINNELL
NEW YORK, NY, 1995
Adopted as fully grown fat cats, Sam, seventeen
pounds, and Dave, fifteen pounds, made their new
owners so happy, they wrote a thank you note to
Bide-A-Wee.

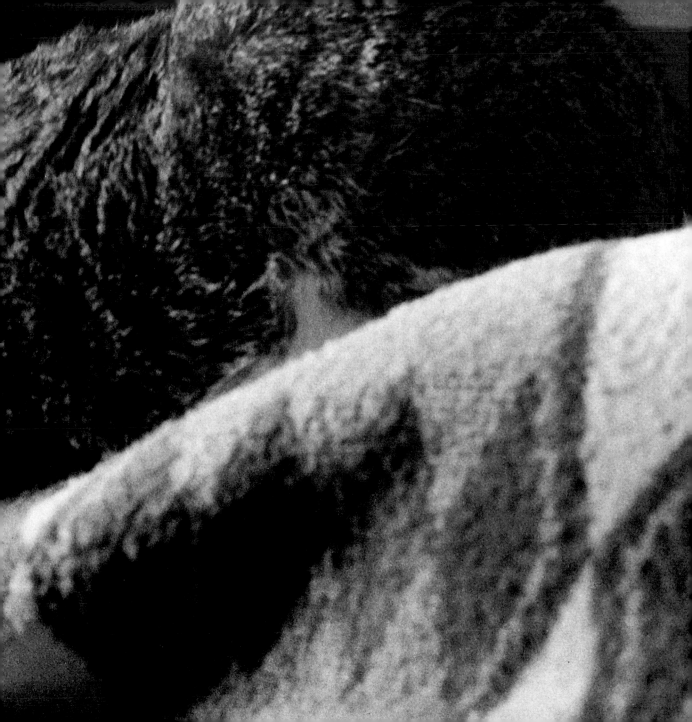

A home without a cat and

a well-fed, well-petted

and properly revered

cat, may be a perfect

home, perhaps, but how

can it prove its title?

MARK TWAIN

THOMAS WESTER
RAMKVILLA, SWEDEN, 1984
"I met this farm woman, Maria, when I was hiking in
the woods of Småland. She obliged me by allowing
me to photograph her seventeen-pound cat."

Cats are always elegant.

JOHN WEITZ
THE ARTISTIC CAT

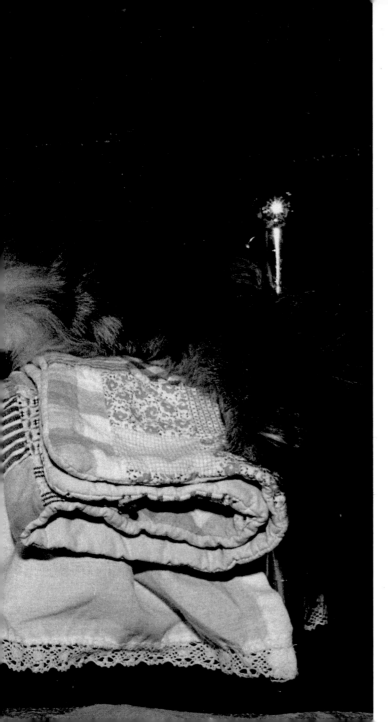

ROBIN SCHWARTZ
NEW YORK, NY, 1994

"A Norwegian Forest cat at the
International Cat Show in
Madison Square Garden.
His name is Billy Joe."

Even overweight cats instinctively

know the cardinal rule: when

fat, arrange yourself in slim poses.

JOHN WITY
CAT QUOTATIONS

CHAIM KANNER
VENICE, ITALY, 1987
"This cat acted like a dog out for a stroll with his
master. He was placid, complacent, and unafraid."

IRVING ROSEN
P·LACE UNKOWN, DATE UNKNOWN

A fat black Persian who seems unaware of her dark beauty.

RIGHT:
JOE CARROLL
GREENSBORO, NC, 1993
Biker Mark Sanders a.k.a "Skidmark"and his pal, Edward
Pfeiffer McIntosh Carrollcat. Edward has slimmed down to
twenty eight pounds from forty since his friends joked that
his stripes had stretch marks.

As anyone who has ever been around

a cat for any length of time well knows,

cats have enormous patience with the

limitations of the human mind.

CLEVELAND AMORY
THE QUOTABLE FELINE

RIGHT:
THOMAS WESTER
SUNDRE, GOTLAND, SWEDEN, 1985
This fat cat weighs in at 15.4 pounds and
loves to amuse himself in the dining room.

OVERLEAF:
KARL BADEN
CAMBRIDGE, MA, 1990
"Ohmie has belonged to a friend for eighteen years. On a
visit to the local animal hospital, despite her girth, the vet,
amazed at what great shape she was in for a cat of her
age, said, 'This cat has the body of a twelve-year-old.'"

JOYCE RAVID
NEW YORK, NY, 1976

"This is fat cat Brother and his 'keeper.'
Brother thinks it is impolite to ask his weight."

The great charm of cats is their rampant

egotism, their devil-may-care attitude

toward responsibility, their disinclination

to earn an honest dollar...cats are disdainful of

everything but their own immediate interests...

ROBERTSON DAVIES
THE PAPERS OF SAMUEL MARCHBANKS

JUST G. MOLLER
JUTLAND, DENMARK, 1959
This fat cat drinks milk from a saucer or a baby
bottle. No matter, as long as lunch is forthcoming.

ABOVE:
NED ROSEN
NEW YORK, NY, 1993

Dinah, Samantha Bowser's very own fat cat, gets her
exercise in an almost supine position.

RIGHT:
NED ROSEN
NEW YORK, NY, 1993

Even if you weigh seventeen pounds, you can still maintain
your dignity, as Dinah proves in this portrait with
Samantha.

PHOTO CREDITS

Cover, 2: Marilaide Ghigliano
Backcover, 7, 8–9: Doreen and Thomas Vyse
5, 22–25, 39, 54–55, 64–65, 66, 75: Courtesy Archive Photos
1, 27, 79: Paul Coughlin/Jim Dratfield Petography, Inc.,
    from *The Quotable Feline*, © 1996 Alfred A. Knopf
11: Antonín Maly
12–13, 16–17, 30–31, 47, 58–59: Robin Schwartz,
    courtesy Sarah Morthlande Gallery, NYC
14, 15: © John Drysdale
19, 20–21, 29, 34–35, 37, 44–45, 51, 63, 69:
    © Thomas Wester
32: Tony Mendoza
33: © Elliott Erwitt/Magnum Photos
40–41: Ann Tomlinson Finnell
43: Mary Ellen Mark
48–49: Jimmy Chen
53: Paul Coughlin/Jim Dratfield Petography, Inc
57, 76–77: Ned Rosen
61: Chaim Kanner
67: Joe Carroll
70–71: Karl Baden
72–73: Joyce Ravid

Text: H.D.R. Campbell
Drawings: J.C. Suarès
Photo Research: Katrina Fried
Design: Tania Garcia